emotional rescue

First published in the UK in 2018
by Studio Press Books,

an imprint of Kings Road Publishing,
part of Bonnier Books UK,
The Plaza, 535 King's Road,
London, SW10 0SZ

www.studiopressbooks.co.uk
www.bonnierbooks.co.uk

Printed Under License ©2018 Emotional Rescue
www.emotional-rescue.com

1 3 5 7 9 10 8 6 4 2

ISBN 978-1-78741-338-2
Printed in Italy

The Wit & Wisdom of
SISTER

STUDIO
PRESS

My Sister wondered whether her friends actually knew her at all?! None of her presents were actually bottles of booze!

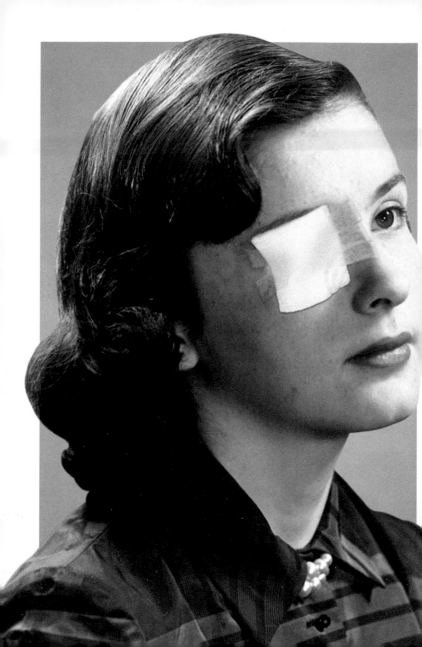

This wasn't quite what Sis meant when she asked for an iPad for her Birthday.

Even from a very early age, she'd constantly found she had 'nothing to wear'!

When her Mum screeched that she treated the house like a hotel, she called reception to complain about the maid's attitude.

Sis knew it was the wrong colour, it didn't fit and it looked like sh*te, but there was 50% off and therefore it had to be bought. Bargain!

"Stop sobbing!" said Mum to my Sister, as she put down her scissors. "It'll soon grow back!!"

Every day, Sis hoped the housework
fairies would come...
but the buggers never did!

When my Sister saw the sign outside the shop saying 'ALL SHOES HALF PRICE' she calmly pulled over.

S is suddenly remembered why she didn't like beans.

Another Birthday disaster as Sis accidentally swallows the 'Happy Birthday' helium balloon.

That was absolutely the last time Sis tried jogging. She'd almost choked on her cake and kept spilling her wine!

Mum didn't have enough money to take her to Alton Towers that year!

S is often communicated with us via instant messaging.

When she was younger, Sis dreamed of growing up, being married to a fabulously wealthy man who would shower her with gifts, hire a maid to cook and clean and be home as little as possible.

S is referred to her age as the 'wonder years'. She'd frequently walk into a room and wonder why she was there.

S is thought there was an outside chance it wasn't iPod compatible.

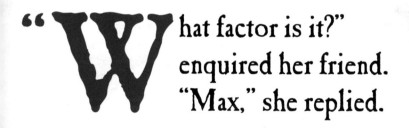

"What factor is it?" enquired her friend. "Max," she replied.

"**B**limey! I went out to celebrate my Birthday after work on Friday night and got totally bladdered, yet this morning I don't seem to have a hangover!" thought Sis, not realising it was now Tuesday.

As she got older, Sis was always walking into things.
Shops, mostly!

Yes she was blonde and no-one was saying that my Sister was thick, but when the instructions said 'Twist to open bottle'...

For my Sister, nothing said 'it's Friday' like a few drinks before the pre-drinks drinks.

My Sister had been gossiping for so long that she couldn't actually prise her fingers off the phone!

Finally, Sis decided to clear out her handbag.

"There's a fab new machine at the gym!" said Sis, "It does absolutely everything! Kit-Kats, Maltesers, crisps..."